Jidoka: The Toyota Principle of Building Quality into the Process

Second Edition

Mohammed Hamed Ahmed Soliman

Published by personal-lean.org, 2020.

JIDOKA: THE TOYOTA PRINCIPLE OF BUILDING QUALITY INTO THE PROCESS

First edition. October 13, 2020.

Second edition. October 7, 2022.

Copyright © 2020 Mohammed Hamed Ahmed Soliman. ISBN: 979-8860279438

Written by Mohammed Hamed Ahmed Soliman.

Table of Contents

Dedication

I created this book with the help of more than fifteen different business resources. These academic articles and books are all cited at the end of this book. A number of people have influenced my learning journey and my entire career. I would like to acknowledge them here. Esraa Soliman: My lovely wife and partner. She encouraged me to write and publish this work. In fact, she always encourages me to do creative work. Jeffrey Liker: Professor at the University of Michigan and author of The Toyota Way and the amazing Toyota series of books. His impressive work on Toyota inspired and influenced my learning about the Toyota Production System. I would really like to thank him for his indirect involvement in this work. Many examples included in this book were originally from his books. Although I have never met Jeff face to face, we have had great communications over social media platforms. Chris Duklet: A lean manufacturing leader from the United States who works in the field of health care. He has contributed to this work by reviewing the book prior to publication and giving me useful recommendations and advice. Attia Gomaa: Professor at the American University in Cairo who influenced my teaching career at the university and taught me how to become a good trainer. Steven Borris: A business consultant, author, and friend from England who influenced my writing career. He encouraged me to write and publish. Steven was my mentor on lean manufacturing, helping me first to understand the basics, after which I developed my understanding through deep practice and self-directed learning. Eslam Soliman: My friend and a professor at the Assiut University. His PhD is from the University of New Mexico. He has influenced my entire writing career by giving me recommendations and advice on how to write and publish. He revised my published works many times and kept inspiring me after every piece I wrote and published.

Jidoka

The Toyota Principle of Building Quality into the Process

Mohammed Hamed Ahmed Soliman

Introduction

Jidoka is one of the main pillars of the TPS. The TPS is presented as a house with two pillars. One pillar represents just-in-time (JIT), and the other pillar the concept of Jidoka. Take away any of the pillars holding up the roof, and the entire system will collapse. Take out quality, and there is no TPS. Jidoka is a principle of building quality for customers—not inspecting quality. Building quality mean making it right the first time. If you are making defective products or using unacceptable quality standards and filtering these defects out through an inspection system, there is no building quality—and no Jidoka. You are just catching the mistakes made in the manufacturing process. This cost a lot of money and resources and puts the business at risk.

Yet many companies focus on the mechanisms of implementation—one-piece flow, pull production, takt time, standard work, kanban—without linking those mechanisms back to the pillars that hold up the entire system. JIT is fairly well understood, but Jidoka is key to making the entire system stick. A lot of failed implementations can be traced back to not building this second pillar.

Going back into history

The principle's origin goes back to 1902 when Sakichi Toyoda invented a simple but ingenious mechanism that detected a broken thread and shut off an automatic loom. That invention allowed one operator to oversee the operation of up to a dozen looms while maintaining perfect quality. But the system goes much further.

Detect and Signal Abnormalities

To build quality into the process machines have to be designed to detect defects when they occur and automatically stop production so an employee can fix a problem before the defect continues downstream.

One of Taiichi Ohno's famous quotes is "get the factory to work for the business the same way the human body works for the person". This is to say that when your body needs more blood, you don't have to tell the heart to pump. It does so autonomically. Jidoka is the concept that you need to design processes and systems so that when errors occur, people respond immediately in support. So, at midnight on a Saturday, how do your systems respond to errors? Do the errors come to light immediately and problem solving begin or does everything wait until Monday? Jidoka would drive you to ensure that abnormalities are made immediately visible at all times and it would drive you to ensure the associates who respond to that abnormality have the capability and authority to fix it.

Toyota uses an andon cords or pull cords which can bring the entire assembly line to halt. Every team member has the authority to stop the line every time they see something out of standard. As Liker explained in Toyota Way, "jidoka referred to as automation-equipment endowed with human intelligent to stop itself when it has a problem."

Jidoka Culture

My first exposure to Jidoka was in a manufacturing company in Egypt that tried to apply this principle to improve quality and safety. In this factory, if you didn't run the production 100% of the shift, you had to explain to the divisions. Quality and preventative maintenance are compromised in favor of quantity. By building a culture of stopping to fix problems, you are encouraging the workforce not to hide their problems that are actually killing profitability and causing inefficiencies. You should be planning for a long-term productivity.

The traditional mass productivity thinking promotes making as many parts as possible using the maximum available resources and all available machines to reduce the cost per piece. The approach assumes higher production numbers equal lower cost per unit. Any problem occurs can be solved later, because there is a lot of inventory buffer that will keep processes working regardless of problems. Problems are not sensible. In mass productivity quality is controlled by additional inspection. Furthermore, if you are making 500 parts, and there was a problem with the production process, a quality failure can occur with all of those parts. Losses will be extremely huge. Problems are also hidden; it will be also so difficult to discover where the error is coming from. So, the root causes will remain hidden.

With lean, production is operating with one-piece flow principle, where stopping one process will stop the others and create a sense of urgency. Everyone is now aware and know we have some problems to fix. We have to work to solve them permanently, or else the line stoppage will be excessive.

JIDOKA: THE TOYOTA PRINCIPLE OF BUILDING QUALITY INTO THE PROCESS

How Jidoka prevents quality problems?

The primary goal of Jidoka is to prevent quality issues from passed to the next process or reaching the customer (which can be a disaster). This is one of the great benefits of lean which work hardly to reduce batch sizes. At the same time, Toyota doesn't aim to lose production or putting the production process at risk. That's why they have built a system of "Minimizing Line Stoppage Time" utilizing problems solving and mistake proofing techniques. Dr Liker presented the problem-solving cycle associate with Jidoka culture in Toyota Way Field book as follow:

1. **Recognizing problems**: standardization is the foundation of quality. Without standard it's difficult to know if there is a problem or not. Without standard everyone will do the work differently which can cause quality problems. Standard work provides a point of comparison. Any problem recognized by the operator should be solved immediately. If can't be solved, the operator must request for help.

2. **Escalating problems:** if the condition is out of control, or problem is not minor, employee must request for support. This is being signaled by pulling the cord which signal the need for assistance. The andon instrument used by Toyota quickly send signals to the designated support people (in Toyota team leaders and group leaders). This typically include buzzer alarm to signal and a visible light to pinpoint location.

3. **Estimate:** the leader must be able to solve the problem within a specific given time period. If he couldn't do this, he must escalate the problem to the higher senior level. Later, leadership must work to solve these issues and prevent the recurrence of same kind of problems. Management role is to

ensure resources, tools, and procedures are provided clearly in the workplace.

4. Control: leadership must tackle the source of problems. Walk through the line and fix the issues permanently. If the source of variation can't be identified, the leadership must take the decision of restarting the line.

5. Eliminating root causes: after controlling the issue and resuming productivity, the team must identify the sources of variation, use PDCA to implement the best countermeasure to prevent the problem from occurring and stopping the line again.

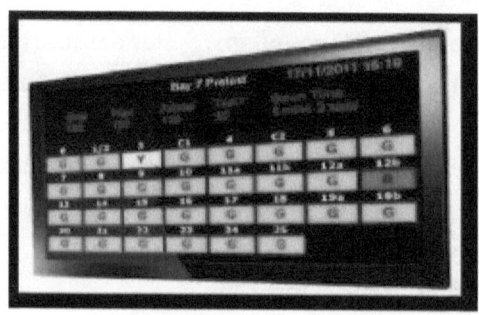

Jidoka is a Principle of Building in Quality not Losing Production!

U nfortunately, and like many other companies there is a wrong misunderstand about the concept and how it operates. As Liker illustrated in The Toyota Way when Toyota competitors started to use the andon system, they made the same mistake of assuming the line-stop system was hardwired to each and every production line. So when the button is pushed, the entire assembly line like comes to a screeching halt. At Toyota, the principle of andon is worked remarkably different. When an operator in a workstation pushes an andon button, that workstation will light up in yellow typically like the traffic light, but the line will continue moving. The team leader has until the product moves into the next workstation zone to respond, before the andon turns red and the line segment automatically stop. As Liker explained, in Toyota this likely is to be a matter of 15-30 seconds on an assembly line making cars at one minute. In that time the team leader might immediately fix the problem or note it can be fixed while the car is moving into other workstations and push the button again, canceling out the line stoppage. Or the team leader might conclude the line should stop.

In that system, that are many considerations and tips presented in The Toyota Way:

1. The team leader has to be trained as well on a standardization procedure on how to respond to andon calls.

2. The assembly line should be divided into segments with small buffers of products in between (in Toyota this buffer is

typically 7-10 cars). Because of the buffer, when a line segment stops, the next line can keep working for about 10 minutes using the buffer and before the entire plant is shut down and rarely does it do shutdown.

3. The purpose of andon is to build in quality, not to lose production. Toyota achieved the purpose of andon without taking needless risks of lost production.

4. Some manufacturers assign a worker to watch the machine for error. This is a waste of the human precise time! Operator that is watching the machine for error is a pure waste and you have to develop a method (like Toyota andon) so problems are surfaced automatically when they occur.

The Two Different Concepts of Jidoka Principle

The first concept is to separate man from machine. It was normal in the original parent company for a single young woman to operate many machines since they were automated. So when Mr. Ohno came to the automotive company after WW II and saw one man operating one machine tool he thought that it was strange and inefficient.

He embarked upon a path of breaking down the notion of one man one machine in the engine shops. Instead of "monitoring" machines the operator was to walk between two machine tools and keep them both up and running. Then three machines and four machines and so on.

The second concept of Jidoka is of course the concept of building in 100% quality every time at the process and not inspecting it in later downstream.

This means you have to have a highly capable process and know how to maintain all the key variables in the process so that a good part is made every time. If a problem occurs the machine should stop right away.

The main purpose of Jidoka principle is to discover quality problems at earlier stages, find the root causes and eliminate the problem from recurring again in the future. By doing so you are saving both your customer and your business. If a defected product is passed to customer so this is a problem and because customers are what keep you in business, you have to build quality for them. This is one of the main lean goals. The goal is to prevent a quality issue that is reducing productivity every day and killing your capacity, decreasing value, increasing costs and reducing safety. Lean encourages you to make it right from first time and this is why surfacing problems is important and can't be done without a single-piece-flow system. Inspecting defects before they pass to the customer is not really the main goal of lean. But having a system that allow information to flow, problems to surface so they can be fixed immediately is the goal. Root causes should be identified and eliminated through kaizen. With lean, there is no or very little inventory buffer, so when process A stops process B will stop too. This allow problems to be noticed quickly and eliminated. There will be no more underlying costs and hidden wastes.

You can't compromise quality. Quality problems are one of the greatest wastes in the process. Quality is what adds value for your customer and keeps you in business and defective products that reach the customer can lead to complete business loss.

Analyzing Quality Failures to Eliminate Root Causes

B asically, it is not difficult to know how many defective products are produced, as a simple sheet of paper can record this information. What is not easy to know is what caused the defects. Finding out can require intensive efforts to understand the source of variation that is causing the quality problem. And this is why one-piece flow improves quality. When problems are quickly noticed, they can be solved and eliminated immediately before they become chronic and costly.

Finding problems in quality is an important function of management. When faced with issues, many practitioners go straight to a complex tool like Six Sigma to find the sources of variation. But often, the simple approach of go and see (referred to gemba) could find the real cause easily. Monitoring how the operator is producing, revising the work against the standard, and involving the technical team could clear up many things. Comparing the machine or process with another one that produces the same part with fewer defects can make the analysis even quicker and easier.

At Toyota, managers use very few complex statistical tools for quality. They usually stick with go and see, mistake proofing techniques, a simple analysis tool like Pareto and problem-solving approaches like the five-whys, as Liker reported in his best-selling book The Toyota Way.

Quality improvement techniques

There are many tools to accomplish the quality goals at every aspect of the process. There are many tools that will help prevent quality problems before they occur and allow you to plan for an error-free product. Poka Yoka which is a Japanese term, also refers to mistake-proofing is an effective tool to prevent human-errors. I have personally used it many times when conducting a failure mode effect analysis process. This tool can improve quality in many business processes include service, manufacturing, and design. Inventory control is another technique that is usually associated with any mistake proofing device.

There are large number of applications in real world regarding the use of mistake proofing in product design. Examples: Limit switches to assure a part correctly placed or fixture before process is performed; part features that only allow assembly the correct way, unique connectors to avoid misconnecting wire harnesses or cables, part symmetry that avoids incorrect insertion.

Unfortunately, companies invest on technologies mistakenly thinking that technology can prevent errors. Technology can only support people and systems to prevent errors when there are good management system and people are trained on problems solving and how to react immediately to abnormalities.

To assess a product failure and determine failure mechanism that need mistake-proofing you may need the use of a technique like failure mode and effect analysis.

Failure mode effect analysis (FMEA) is a process of assessing the failure risk based on its occurrence, severity, and detectability. The more detectable methods we have in the system to detect and predict failure, the lower the risk of the product failure. FMEA and if used properly, can be a good tool in improving quality. An article that I wrote and published in the

JIDOKA: THE TOYOTA PRINCIPLE OF BUILDING QUALITY INTO THE PROCESS

Industrial Management magazine "Analyzing Failure to Prevent Problems" can illustrate this as well. Many organizations only use FMEA during the design stage, but FMEA can be really used in manufacturing, design, service and maintenance.

Lean is not a toolkit for manufacturing to lower costs for profitability. Lean is a long-term strategy to satisfy customers through better quality and lower costs. Engineering a product that solve your customer's usage problems is a legitimate lean goal. Lean is about innovation and creativity. If you can manufacture defect-free product or build quality into the design, this will help satisfy customers and increase their confidence.

Cost of Quality

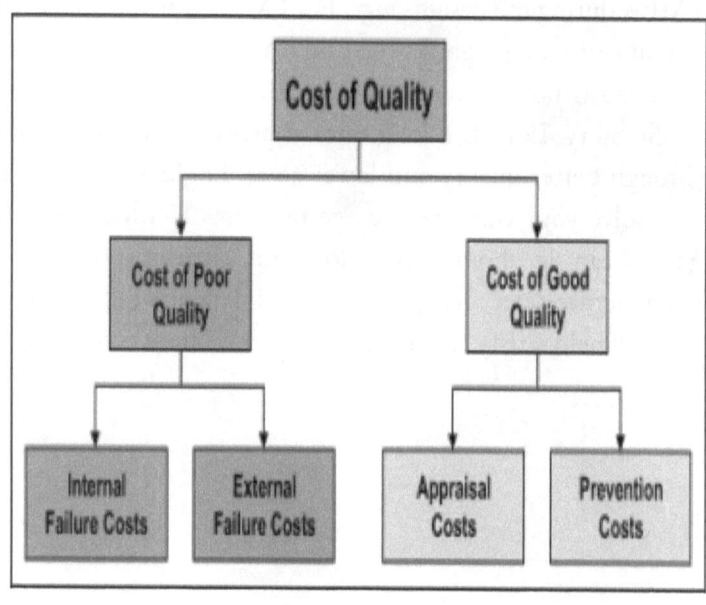

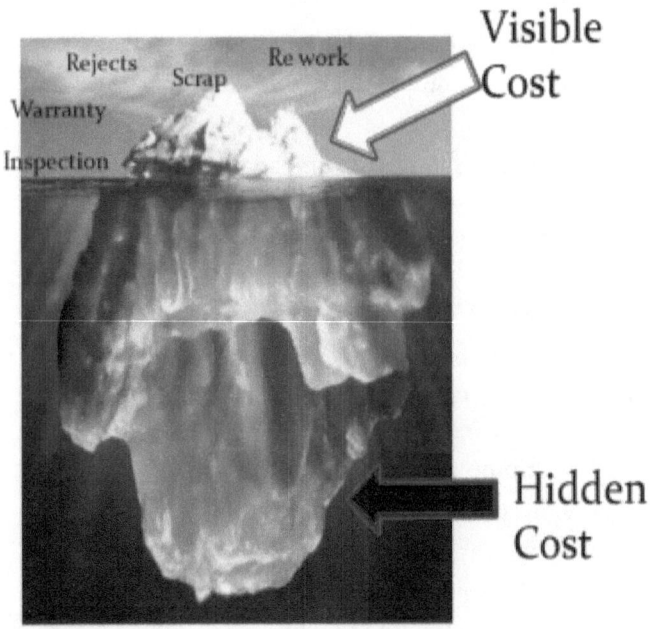

Usually high percent of the actual costs are hidden

Cost of Poor Quality: Internal Failure Costs

Internal failure costs are costs that are caused by products or services not conforming to requirements or customer/user needs and are found before delivery of products and services to external customers. They would have otherwise led to the customer not being satisfied. Deficiencies are caused both by errors in products and inefficiencies in processes. Examples include the costs for:

- Rework.
- Delays.
- Re-designing.
- Shortages.

- Failure analysis.
- Re-testing.
- Downgrading.
- Downtime.
- Lack of flexibility and adaptability.

Cost of Poor Quality: External Failure Costs

External failure costs are costs that are caused by deficiencies found after delivery of products and services to external customers, which lead to customer dissatisfaction. Examples include the costs for:

- Complaints.
- Repairing goods and redoing services.
- Warranties.
- Customers' bad will.
- Losses due to sales reductions.
- Environmental costs.

It takes 1-3 years to re compensate a leaving customer

Cost of Good Quality: Prevention Costs

Prevention costs are costs of all activities that are designed to prevent poor quality from arising in products or services. Examples include the costs for:

- Quality planning.

JIDOKA: THE TOYOTA PRINCIPLE OF BUILDING QUALITY INTO THE PROCESS

- Supplier evaluation.
- New product review.
- Error proofing.
- Capability evaluations.
- Quality improvement team meetings.
- Quality improvement projects.
- Quality education and training.

Cost of Good Quality: Appraisal Costs

Appraisal costs are costs that occur because of the need to control products and services to ensure a high-quality level in all stages, conformance to quality standards and performance requirements. Examples include the costs for:

- Checking and testing purchased goods and services.
- In-process and final inspection/test.
- Field testing.
- Product, process or service audits.
- Calibration of measuring and test equipment.

Appendix I. Toyota Recalls Crisis

JIDOKA: THE TOYOTA PRINCIPLE OF BUILDING QUALITY INTO THE PROCESS

Recall Issue	Myth	Reality	Cause
Pedal entrapped by unsecured or incompatible floor mate	Carpet design causes pedal entrapment, leading to accidents and deaths	No defects exists with properly installed floor mat. Floor mats that are unsecured, stacked or incompatible have the potential to entrap the accelerator pedal. Also true for other auto makers	Improper use of floor mates
Sticking accelerator pedal	Pedal frequently gets stuck leading to uncontrollable acceleration and causing many accidents	In rare cases, pedal can get sticky and return slowly to idle or temporarily stick partially depressed. There were no causes of wide-open throttle. In all cases, brakes will stop car in normal stopping distance	As a result of heat, humidity, or condensation, synthetic material in pedal become sticky. Braking performance is not affected

JIDOKA: THE TOYOTA PRINCIPLE OF BUILDING QUALITY INTO THE PROCESS

Recall Issue	Myth	Reality	Cause
Electronic throttle control system failure	Electromagnetic interference or software glitches cause runaway cars that will not stop in a way peculiar to Toyota's design has lead to accidents and even deaths.	This change has been made against all car companies, and there has never been evidence of a single case. Millions of hours of tests by Toyota in chambers that generate EMI and in real world tests in high EMI-areas have never revealed a single instance	No confirmed problem
2010 Prius ABS problem	On slippery roads, brakes can stop working, severely affecting braking performance .	At speeds below 35mph on slippery or bumpy surfaces, switch from re generative to ABS braking system causes the brake pedal to momentarily feel soft. There is no impact on braking performance	The software governing the braking system does not provide proper feel in the braking pedal

Engineering Errors Leading to Recalls: Myths and Reality (Liker and Ogden, 2010)

• • • •

MOHAMMED HAMED AHMED SOLIMAN

"The Rate of Growth was higher than the Rate of People Development"
Akio Toyoda, President of Toyota Company

LESSONS TO LEARN FROM Toyota Crisis:

1. Your crises responses started yesterday
2. A Culture of Responsibility will always beat a culture of finger pointing.
3. Even the best vulture develops weaknesses.
4. Developing your people is an endless cycle.

Appendix II. Standard Work

If no standardization, then no quality. Everyone will do this task differently. Tracking the source of errors is difficult without standardization (Ahmed, 2014). When a leader performs gemba walk on shop floor to observe the situation, there is no benefit from the walk when there is no standard (Ahmed, 2014 and Soliman, 2020).

Standard work refers to the standard way in which any value-adding job need to be done. The standard involves the work, the work sequence, the tools needed, the equipment needed, the material needed, and the amount of time it should take.

Establishing a standard is the foundation of continuous improvement. If there is no standard, how will I know whether I have improved or not? Also, if the job is not being done the same way every time, how can we get consistent quality and productivity? (Ahmed, 2014).

Standard must be established for each work assigned to the operator in the cell. It can be made and posted on the wall so each one now knows the work, the sequence, and the time require to do the job. Standard must be established also for changeover tasks. If you want to reduce setup times, you have to standardize the setup tasks.

Without clear standards, it is difficult for a manager to get much out of a gemba visit (Soliman, 2020). The more established the standards, the more productive the visit. Companies that want to develop their leaders should use a board for standardized work by assigning cards for each job on the production line, each organized by job number in the area, including a map. The cards should have the following yes-no questions:

- Is the standardized work chart accurate in its times?
- Is the takt correct?
- Is the operator following the steps in sequence?
- Is the operator following the steps in timing?
- Are all the key points being followed?

Each day, the group leader should take one card, pull the job breakdown sheet and observe, looking for deviations from standardized work. Any deviations lead to an answer of "No" and should include a written explanation (Soliman, 2016). The managers also should randomly pick a card each day and do the same thing. In the case of any differences, the managers would go through the job with the group leader. This is highly effective. It assumes you are building to takt and following standardized work, at least to a degree, and that everything is kept reasonably up to date. It's highly unusual for everyone to follow standard work perfectly, so there should be observed deviations that will lead to problem-solving.

Getting people to follow the standard is not that easy job. Most focus tend to be on the end results not on the way things have to be done. For example, producing 500 pieces in a shift, as long as managers get the 500 pieces, they are happy. Therefore, getting people to follow the standard is one of the hardest jobs in lean transformation. Here are some tips in getting people involved: (Soliman, 2016 and Ahmed, 2013).

JIDOKA: THE TOYOTA PRINCIPLE OF BUILDING QUALITY INTO THE PROCESS

1. Allow employee to share their own ideas for improving their own works. This will make the employee feel themselves and that they are valuable to the process.

2. Employee should consider the improvement an enjoyable part of their work rather than a new method to follow. Giving people a degree of autonomy will increase the self-motivation and encourage them to participate and follow what they have contributed in.

3. People should believe in the process and that they are doing the improving for their work to become easier, and safer not to get rewarded. They should be allowed to share and put their own ideas under a self-motivated and cooperative system to improve their own works.

4. When you are on the shop floor and observing the work, introduce yourself and explain what you are doing. Don't take notes in the front the production associates without showing them what you have written. Explain always that you are observing the process not the people. We call these actions shop floor courtesy.

5. When it is so difficult to get people involved due to the culture of the organization, it will be ok to put a little pressure on people to force them begin the improvement and work with a standard, but you have to make sure that they do believe that this standard is better for their work, their safety, the quality and the overall company's performance. Also, you can only initiate the process and you must give them a degree of freedom to modify this standard and continuously improvement it.

Peer in mind that standardized work for a factory floor is something that can't be created at a desk in the engineering offices; it must be defined and revised at the gemba. And engineering managers know that standardization of work is the foundation for quality and continuous improvement (Ahmed, 2014).

Unfortunately, some engineers and consultants try to implement standard operating procedures created at offices or brought from other companies. Such external SOPs must be adapted, modified and improved to match the company's current situation and process conditions (Soliman, 2020). Besides, pushing SOPs without getting the front-line people involved in sharing ideas for improvement will end with a process failure. Workers must contribute to creating those SOPs. They should believe that the standardization of work is not an order to follow but rather something to facilitate their work, making it easier and safer (Liker, 2012).

For example, standardization of the operator work in a cell must be performed at the gemba (Soliman, 2020). It is still difficult to watch the operator and measure the time in front of him so don't forget the shop floor courtesy.

When observing the operator work and measuring the time in a cell to create a standard work for the operator, consider the following (Soliman, 2020 and Rother, 2009):

1. Don't rely on reports
2. Don't rely on previous time studies recorded at the engineering office
3. Don't rely on any past time study
4. Measure each work element separately not the total time required by an operator to perform a sequence of work elements.
5. Don't include any walk as a work element

JIDOKA: THE TOYOTA PRINCIPLE OF BUILDING QUALITY INTO THE PROCESS

6. Don't include out of cycle work for operators as work elements. eg, moving to get parts, quality checks, moving containers.
7. Don't include operators waiting for machines to cycle as a work element.
8. Don't include time for removing finished parts from machines wherever you believe automatic eject could reasonably be introduced.
9. Separate the machine time from operator time.
10. Get the operator involved in what you are going to do.

Standard and Quality

Variation in quality or poor quality can be triggered back to a standardization issue. The operator has to be working according to the standard, operating machine according to the standard and using the raw material specs according to the standard.

As defined by Liker (2005), there are two types of standard concern quality:

- Standard Specifications: this includes dimension, tolerance, processing methods, equipment operation condition (pressure, temp. etc.) and parameters and corrective action information.
- Standard procedures: this includes the instructions, standard work process, kanban rules, material flow, production boards, color coding and 5S.

Jidoka principle which is the second pillar of Toyota production system, bring the line to halt to avoid passing quality issues to the next stage (Soliman, 2020). They use andon cords to discover errors and immediately take actions. The instructions about how to react and take decisions must be standardized (Soliman, 2016).

Kanban cards (pull cards) used to regulate production between lines, between the supplier and the process and between the process and the customer must have all information standardized (Liker, 2003 and Liker, 2005).

Appendix III. FMEA

FMEA is a systematic method for identifying and preventing product and process problems before they occur. FMEAs are focused on preventing defects, enhancing safety and increasing customer satisfaction.

FMEAs are conducted in the product design or process development stages, although conducting an FMEA on existing products and processes can also yield substantial benefits.

What is the purpose of a FMEA?

Preventing the process and product problems before they occur is the purpose of Failure Mode Effect Analysis. Used in both the design and manufacturing process, they substantially reduce costs by identifying product and process improvement early in the develop process when changes are relativity easy and inexpensive to make.

• • • •

FMEA CAN PROVIDE THE answer to many problems:

How can we prevent this problem from occurring again in the future?

How can we minimize the risk of this potential failure?

How can we produce an error-free product?

How can we reduce the warranty costs?

How can we improve the safety condition in the workplace?

FMEA as a part of a Comprehensive Quality System

Can FMEA be used alone? While FMEAs can be effectively used alone, a company won't get maximum benefit without systems to support conducting FMEAs.

Two things are necessary needed:

1. A reliable product or process data. Without this data, FMEA becomes a guessing game based on opinions rather than actual facts. Without data the team may focus on the wrong failure modes or missing significant opportunities to improve the failure modes that are the biggest problems.
2. Documentation of procedures. In the absence of documents and procedures, people working in the process could be introducing significant variation in to it by operating it slightly different each time the process is run.

Benefits of Failure Modes Effect Analysis "FMEA"

The object of an FMEA is to look for all of the ways a process or product can fail. A product failure occurs when the product does not function as it should or when it malfunctions in some way.

Contribute to improve design for product & process
- Higher reliability.
- Better Quality.
- Increase Safety.

Contribute to cost saving
- Decrease development time & redesign cost.
- Decrease warranty costs.
- Decrease wastes.

Contribute to continuous improvement

FMEA Applies to: System, Process, Design, and Service

JIDOKA: THE TOYOTA PRINCIPLE OF BUILDING QUALITY INTO THE PROCESS

FMEA helps manufacturing engineers control the process and eliminate errors during production, thus decreasing warranty costs and wastes.

Service engineers use FMEA to improve the lifecycle of the product and lower its service costs by developing a proper maintenance program.

Potential Applications:
- Equipment components & parts.
- Component proving process.
- Outsourcing/resourcing of product.
- Develop suppliers to achieve quality.
- Major process/ Equipment / Technology Changes.

- Cost Reductions.
- New Product/ Design Analysis.
- Assist in analysis in a flat Pareto chart.

Failure Mode – example to failure modes

- Any event which causes a functional failure.
- Ways in which product or process can fail are called failure modes. The FMEA is a way to identify the failures, effects, and risks within a process or product, and then eliminate or reduce them.

Example failure modes:
- Bearing Seized.
- Motor burned out.
- Coupling broken.
- Impeller jammed.

<u>Compressors Failure Modes</u>

Discharge pressure low:
- Air leakage.
- leaking valves.
- Defect gauge.

<u>Engines Failures Mode</u>

Knocking:
- Pistons hitting the head.
- Crankshaft plays.
- Oil pump not function.

Example failure modes, coffee maker

Indeed, even the plain devices have numerous chances for failures. For instance, a trickle espresso producer. A relativity basic family unit machine could have a few things bomb that would deliver the coffeemaker inoperable. Here are a few different ways the espresso make can fizzle:

- The warming component doesn't warm water to adequate temperature to mix espresso.
- The siphon doesn't siphon water into the channel container.
- The espresso producer doesn't turn on consequently by the clock.
- The clock quits working or running excessively quick or excessively moderate.
- There is a short in the electrical rope.
- There is either insufficient or an excessive amount of espresso utilized.

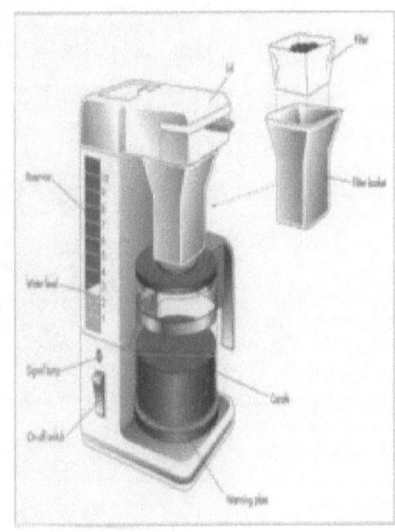

THE GOAL IS:
100%
Customer
Satisfaction

Failures are not limited to problems with the product. Because failures also can occur when the user makes a mistake. Those types of failures should be included in the FMEA. Anything can be done to ensure the product works correctly, regardless of how the user operates it, will move the product closer to 100 percent total customer satisfaction.

JIDOKA: THE TOYOTA PRINCIPLE OF BUILDING QUALITY INTO THE PROCESS

Failure Effects Description

<u>Local Effect</u>

The failure effect as it applies to the item under analysis.

Ex. Water pump stop.

<u>Next Higher Effect</u>

The failure effect as it applies at the next higher indenture level.

Ex. Water system pressure drop down.

<u>End-Effect</u>

The failure effect at the highest indenture level or total system.

Ex. System stop.

Appendix V. Problems Solving Using non-statistical tools

5 Whys

5 whys is a method of tackling the root cause of the problem and prevent recurrent failure. It was originated in Japan. Japanese people believe that by asking 5 whys you can figure out the root cause of the problem and find the solution. However, it doesn't have to be 5 it can be 7 or 8.

Toyota

Toyota does not have a six-sigma program. Six sigma is based on complex statistical quality analysis tools. It is a surprise for people to realize how Toyota has achieved this level of quality without the use of six sigma for quality.

Most of problems don't call for complex statistical analysis, but instead require detailed problem solving. This requires a level of detailed thinking and analysis that is all too absent from most companies in day-to-day activities.

JIDOKA: THE TOYOTA PRINCIPLE OF BUILDING QUALITY INTO THE PROCESS

	Level of Problem	Countermeasure
	There is an oil on the shop floor	Clean up the oil
Why?	Because the machine is leaking	Fix the machine
Why?	Because the gasket has deteriorated	Replace the gasket
Why?	Because we bought gaskets made of inferior material	Change gasket specifications
Why?	Because we got a good deal/price on those gaskets	Change purchasing policy
Why?	Because the purchasing gets evaluated on short-term cost saving	Change the evaluation policy for purchasing agent

5 whys is a method to pursue the deeper, systematic causes of a problem to find correspondingly deeper countermeasures

Toyota Practical Problem-Solving Process

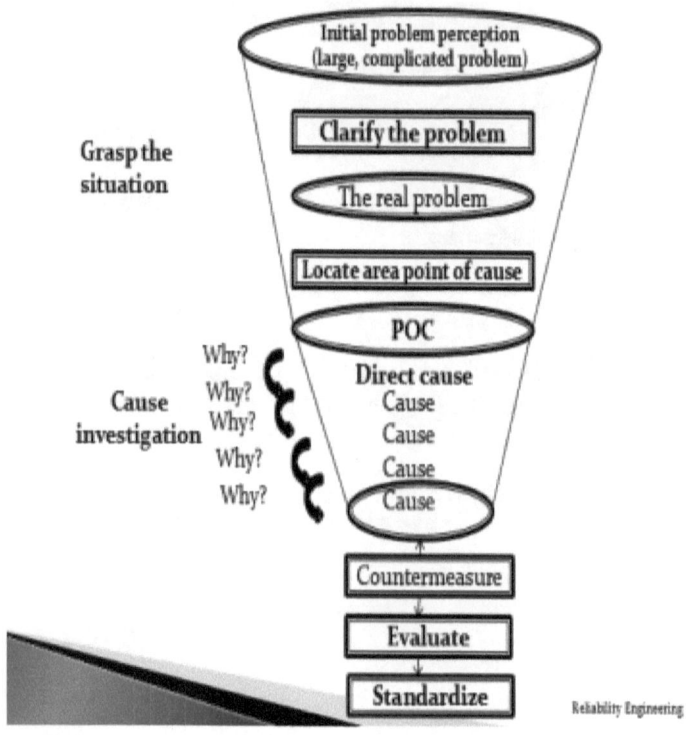

Q1: Why did the customer not buy the product?

A: The salesperson did not persuade him to buy.

Q2: Why did the salesperson not persuade the customer to buy?

A: The salesperson was not good enough.

Q3: Why was the salesperson not good enough?

A: The sales person has not been trained in sales.

Q4: Why has the salesperson not been trained in sales?

A: It was not considered necessary.

Q5: Why was training not considered necessary?

A: Sales are only a small part of the job.

EXAMPLE:

Drawing Cause and Effect Diagram (Fishbone Diagram)

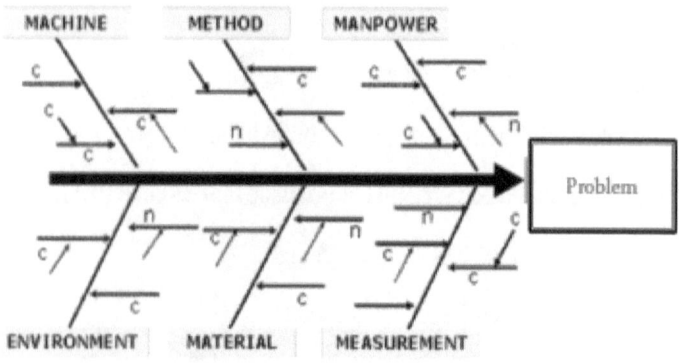

Using a fishbone diagram while brainstorming possible causes helps

you to focus on the various possibilities. Some useful categories:

The main problem is entered in the nose. The bones originally had only "4Ms". Once all problems were reduced to one of the four: man, machine, material, or method. Eventually, measurement was added to highlight how critical it is to have an understanding of the reliability and accuracy of the measuring system. Environment was added to make people consider the location of an equipment and the impact of its surroundings on the operation. Design and instruction can also be a good reason to add. Fishbone diagram take inputs from brainstorming sessions. Those possible countermeasures are the ideas that people give during the brainstorming sessions. Dig deep into the details at the Gemba (the place where real work happens) is necessary to absorb the real situation, perform diagnosis, make analysis, talk to people that are involved directly in the work and base the solution on facts.

Appendix IV. What Toyota's Production System Is Really About

Many people don't understand the DNA of the Toyota Production System and the core values of the Toyota Way. I have seen many who think about the TPS as a tool kit or lean manufacturing techniques that only work with Toyota because Toyota has a different process, a stable environment, or less fluctuation in customer demand. Others believe the TPS works only in the automotive industry.

Jeff K. Liker came out with a remarkable series of books starting with *The Toyota Way* (2003) and ending with *The Toyota Way to Lean Leadership* (Liker and Convis 2012). He revealed the real TPS based on his thirty-plus years of experience studying Toyota. It took him seven books to explain and decode the TPS. It is a Thinking Production System. It is neither a waste removal tool nor a lean manufacturing tactic. Liker presented very well the leadership model behind the system's success.

The TPS is really not what many think. So, what is TPS?

TPS Is a Thinking Production System

When a company says the TPS didn't work for them, it is a leadership failure. I suspect they tried to use the tools rigidly. The tools are flexible, adaptable, and implementable in many different conditions and industries. That's why you have to think about the tools and use your mind. Develop your people and motivate them to think and act.

TPS Is a Long-Term Innovation Process

Without innovation, Toyota would have never have succeeded in anything. Toyota's R&D department has played a major role in Toyota's success. For example, the Toyota wiring loom has gone through several major improvements and developments. The Toyota Prius was the first hybrid vehicle. *Minomi* is a revolution in the material movement. For those who don't know minomi, it is an innovation initiated in Japan. It is focused on eliminating containers completely. One of the Toyota companies in Japan (Central Motors) successfully created a revolution in material flow through a well-designed system to move parts without containers. The system is called minomi. The details are in *The Toyota Way to Lean Leadership* by Liker and Convis (2012).

TPS Is a Customizable Production System

The TPS system can't be copied. What has worked in one environment or specific industry might not work in another. Even from one Toyota plant to another, the system can't be copied identically. You have to think and adapt the tools. You must tailor them to your needs to suit the current conditions. The best example comes from the minomi system. When the Toyota plant in Georgetown, Kentucky, tried to copy and paste the technique from the Japanese plant, the process failed. Later, Gary Convis, the president of the Kentucky plant, led the implementation of the new method using the Toyota Way. They had success because Gary was trained very well in lean thinking. This leads again to the first point. The TPS is a Thinking Production System. The real point is to make people think, and the system won't succeed without leaders trained on lean thinking and lean culture.

TPS Is a Productivity Improvement System

The TPS is not only for manufacturing. The TPS gives outstanding results in any area in which you want to achieve overall improvement in productivity, quality, safety, and reliability. It works very well with many different industries and businesses, and that includes health care, hotels, banking, construction, and more. The problem with the word "production" is that it makes many people think the system is for manufacturing. What about accelerating the check-in and check-out processes in a hotel? Won't this improve productivity and customer experience? There are many success stories outside of manufacturing industries presented in various lean references. However, people somehow managed to ignore the whole-system aspect of lean thinking and started calling it "lean" or "lean manufacturing" instead. This reduction in scope allowed business leaders to dismiss lean as a manufacturing idea. As a result, manufacturing companies believed lean could be delegated, and nonmanufacturing companies believed lean didn't apply to them at all.

TPS Is the Toyota Problem-Solving Kata

Yes, Toyota has its own unique way of solving problems and developing leaders. As mentioned in chapter 6, Toyota has a psychology of process improvement unlike its competitors. *The Toyota Kata* by Mike Rother (2009) provides an excellent example of this routine.

The Deming cycle (PDCA) is a learning cycle rather than a process-improvement cycle. If you solve the problem but don't develop your people, the process will fail. People will not be able to continue managing the process in the new way if they haven't been trained in the culture of continuous improvement. Things will slip back, and it will be difficult to sustain the lean results. This is the problem in many companies.

TPS Is Toyota's People and Systems

People built, modified, and improved this system. People are the foundation of continuous improvement. People are more important than the process, and companies should give higher priority to developing their people and providing excellent working environments for them. Unfortunately, many companies say they do lean, Six Sigma, and other improvement projects to boost morale and develop new routines of thinking. However, they are actually focusing only on the processes and seeking quick outcomes. Toyota is highly committed to leadership development and training and coaching their employees. In *Toyota Under Fire* by Liker and Ogden (2010), when Liker interviewed Akio Toyoda after several recall crises, Mr. Toyoda said the rate of growth had been higher than the rate of people development.

TPS Is a System to Build Quality for Customers

Jidoka is one of the main pillars of the TPS. The TPS is represented like a roof. Take away any of the pillars holding up the roof, and the system will collapse. Take out quality, and there is no TPS. Jidoka is a principle of building quality for customers—not inspecting quality. Building quality mean making it right the first time. If you are making defective products or using unacceptable quality standards and filtering these defects out through an inspection system, there is no building quality—and no jidoka. You are just catching the mistakes made in the manufacturing process. This costs a lot of money and resources and puts the business at risk if a defective product passes to the customer. Quality is what keeps any organization in business.

TPS Is a Strategy

JIDOKA: THE TOYOTA PRINCIPLE OF BUILDING QUALITY INTO THE PROCESS

The TPS is a strategy for excellence. The TPS is a strategy to achieve the goals of excellence in quality, productivity, costs, safety, and morale (Liker and Trachilis 2015). Without a vision aligned with the strategic objectives and stretch goals, the improvement effort will have no direction. The hoshin kanri process will help align the goals, plans, and efforts toward a common goal in order to achieve strategic business objectives. Hoshin kanri pays attention to the method rather than the results—unlike other traditional management approaches, such as MBO. Hoshin kanri focuses on innovative methods for achieving targets under a highly motivational developmental system.

TPS Is Total Performance Solutions

If used properly, these tools can turn around any organization. Speed kills competition. All the tools you need to maximize your productivity, quality, speed, and deliveries are included in the TPS. You just need to learn how to use these tools and implement the culture required to use them in your organization. Remember, a good culture will last forever. A good tool kit under a stressed management system will die quickly. It is all about leadership and how you are going to use these tools.

TPS Is Not Lean

Yes, people called it an inventory reduction program when they first heard of it. "Just in time" is one of the main pillars in the TPS. "Just in time" ideally means "one-piece flow." Inventory is the greatest waste in the process, and it hides many problems, such as quality problems, breakdown times, waiting waste, and more. Let's get back to history. Prior to the 1970 oil crisis, very few people in the world know what Toyota was up to. The fact that it emerged stronger than ever while many of its competitors were quite battered made people take notice. People went to Japan to find out how Toyota had done this. What people found was that Toyota was doing something called "just in time." In the West, this was interpreted as an inventory reduction program. As a result, it became known as the "just-in-time inventory" program. Nobody really believed inventory could be taken out of the whole value stream. Therefore, "just in time" came to mean "go beat the heck out of your suppliers." The big three auto companies (Ford, General Motors, and Chrysler) had lots of power over their suppliers, and they became pretty expert at this tactic—to their eventual detriment. James P. Womack came forward with *Lean Thinking* in 1996 and helped many to see the whole value chain. He showed how waste clogs the system and how continuous improvement was needed to link all parts of the chain to customer demand. He explained his findings in plain English, but once again people didn't hear. Lean might be an element of the larger strategy, but it is most likely to be relegated to plant and manufacturing work. As a result, one company after another has tried lean and failed.

TPS Is Not a Translated Production System

Many techniques used today (with awareness or not) have Japanese names. This includes techniques such as *poka yoke*, hoshin kanri, genchi genbutsu, and others. The TPS is not a documented process. It can, therefore, be translated via people in Japan and the United States and passed through different cultures. Taiichi Ohno refused at the beginning to document the TPS for fear that people would narrowly focus on tools and theories. He said to write it would be to kill it. For example, "genchi genbutsu," or gemba, is translated as "go and see." Leaders, however, will only go and see when there is a problem.

Gemba is being used only as a problem-solving process. As presented in chapter 2, gemba is a place for teaching and learning management. Gemba is the place where value-creating work happens and where you should put value for your customers. All lean tools and techniques, such as value stream mapping, work-standardization processes, and more, must be planned, measured, adapted, standardized, and improved at the workplace. Gemba is a place to solve problems by grasping the current situation and finding the root causes of problems by asking the five whys.

TPS Is a Pull System—Not a Kanban System

A pull system is the key to avoiding overproduction waste. You are linking the chain to customer demand instead of a schedule. You are no longer producing based on a schedule. As presented in *The Toyota Way*, kanban is an organized system of inventory buffers. According to Ohno, inventory is a waste, so kanban is something to strive to get rid of—not be proud of.

TPS Is Not Making to Order in Sequence

The TPS promotes leveling rather than making to order in sequence. Most suppliers try to follow the lean principle of making to order. However, since customer demands are never stable and are naturally unpredictable, irregular, and significantly varied, following the customer demand in sequence can cause a lot of issues and waste. You have to level the product volume and type. That's why many businesses have difficulties building to order. This is also why they say Toyota has a stable environment and less fluctuation in customer demand and why the TPS is only suitable for Toyota. They don't understand the underlying power of leveling.

TPS Is an Eight-Step Toyota Business Practice

There are eight steps in Toyota's business practice when solving problems. As mentioned in chapter 2, Toyota uses PDCA as a routine for learning. The plan stage is invoked five times to ensure the root cause of the problem has been eliminated. Lean emphasizes the plan. The plan phase cannot be created without a daily observation at the gemba to find the root causes of problems, gather facts, discuss things with the process operators, and develop the best countermeasure from different alternatives.

TPS Is Not Zero Inventory

Many think just-in-time inventory means zero inventory. The ideal thing is one-piece flow, and this can only be established through a production cell. There is an inventory buffer, but it is not often used. There is a buffer in the Andon[1] system. There is a buffer to protect your customer. There is a buffer to avoid stopping the whole production line to fix a problem. There is a buffer to avoid breaking down a critical manufacturing process.

TPS Is Built on Deep Supplier Relationships

This is one of the most important factors in Toyota's success. It was explained in chapter 3, which discussed teamwork and Toyota's core values. Few companies realize the importance of working with your suppliers to improve your own process and the value you provide to your customers. If you are not working with your suppliers to truly reduce inventory holdings, the process will fail. If you are trying to reduce inventory and ask your supplier to deliver smaller batch sizes more frequently, and if your supplier is not ready, the process will fail. I have seen many companies trying to shift the costs of holding inventory to their suppliers. This offers no real savings in the complete value stream! You are redistributing the cost to suppliers, but there are no real savings. Very few people understand this. I recommend reading *Building Deep Supplier Relationships* from the Harvard Business Review (Liker and Choi 2004). Building these kinds of relations with suppliers is one of the most difficult parts of implementing the TPS, but it is also the most important part.

References:

Liker, J. K. 2003. The Toyota Way: 14 Management Principles from the World's Greatest Manufacturer. New York: McGraw-Hill.

Liker, J. K., and D. Meier. 2005. The Toyota Way Fieldbook: A Practical Guide for Implementing Toyota's 4Ps. New York: McGraw-Hill.

Rother, M. 2009. The Toyota Kata: Managing People for Improvement, Adaptiveness and Superior Results. New York: McGraw-Hill.

Soliman, M. H. A. 2014. "Analyzing Failure to Prevent Problems." Industrial Management 56 (5): 10.

Womack, J. P., and Jones, D.T. (1996). Lean Thinking: Banish Waste and Create Wealth in Your Corporation. Free Press.

Soliman, M. H. A. 2013. OEE Can Be Your Key: Change Formula for Equipment Availability to Improve Performance. Industrial Engineer 45 (8): 43.

Liker, J. K., and T. N. Ogden. 2010. Toyota Under Fire: Lessons for Turning Crisis into Opportunity. New York: McGraw-Hill.

JIDOKA: THE TOYOTA PRINCIPLE OF BUILDING QUALITY INTO THE PROCESS

About the Author

Mohammed Hamed Ahmed Soliman is an industrial engineer, consultant, university lecturer, operational excellence leader, and author. He works as a lecturer at the American University in Cairo and as a consultant for several international industrial organizations.

Soliman earned a bachelor of science in Engineering and a master's degree in Quality Management. He earned post-graduate degrees in Industrial Engineering and Engineering Management. He holds numerous certificates in management, industry, quality, and cost engineering.

For most of his career, Soliman worked as a regular employee for various industrial sectors. This included crystal-glass making, fertilizers, and chemicals. He did this while educating people about the culture of continuous improvement.

Soliman has lectured at Princess Noura University and trained the maintenance team in Vale Oman Pelletizing Company. He has been lecturing at The American University in Cairo for 6 year and has designed and delivered 40 leadership and technical skills enhancement training modules.

Soliman is a member at the Institute of Industrial and Systems Engineers and a member with the Society for

Engineering and Management Systems. He has published several articles in peer reviewed academic journals and magazines. His writings on lean manufacturing, leadership, productivity, and business appear in Industrial Engineers, Lean Thinking, and Industrial Management. Soliman's blog is www.personal-lean.org.

Also, by Soliman

MOHAMMED HAMED AHMED SOLIMAN

JIDOKA: THE TOYOTA PRINCIPLE OF BUILDING QUALITY INTO THE PROCESS

[1] The Andon system is a part of the Toyota principle of building quality for customers (jidoka) and refers to the use of an alarm system on the production line to prevent defects from passing to the next process.

Don't miss out!

Visit the website below and you can sign up to receive emails whenever Mohammed Hamed Ahmed Soliman publishes a new book. There's no charge and no obligation.

https://books2read.com/r/B-A-VCQM-XHVBC

BOOKS 2 READ

Connecting independent readers to independent writers.

Did you love *Jidoka: The Toyota Principle of Building Quality into the Process*? Then you should read *Takt Time: A Guide to the Very Basic Lean Calculation* by Mohammed Hamed Ahmed Soliman!

Takt time is calculated as the amount of manufacturing time that is available divided by the volume of orders. In the 1930s, the German aviation industry employed Takt for the first time as a production management tool. The idea was widely used within Toyota in the 1950s, and by the late 1960s, it had been adopted by the majority of the Toyota supplier base. Every month, Toyota assesses the takt for a process, with a modifying review occurring every 10 days. Takt time is used to properly balance supply and demand. It gives a lean production system its beating heart.

Read more at https://www.personal-lean.org/.

Also by Mohammed Hamed Ahmed Soliman

5S: A Practical Guide to Visualizing and Organizing Workplaces to Improve Productivity

Hoshin Kanri: How Toyota Creates a Culture of Continuous Improvement to Achieve Lean Goals

Industrial Applications of Infrared Thermography: How Infrared Analysis Can be Used to Improve Equipment Inspection

The Seven Deadly Wastes and How to Remove Them from Your Business: The Heart of the Toyota Production System

Ultrasound Analysis for Condition Monitoring: Applications of Ultrasound Detection for Various Industrial Equipment

Manufacturing Wastes Stream: Toyota Production System Lean Principles and Values

Takt Time: A Guide to the Very Basic Lean Calculation

Toyota Standard Work: The Foundation of Kaizen

Jidoka: The Toyota Principle of Building Quality into the Process

Machine Reliability and Condition Monitoring: A Comprehensive Guide to Predictive Maintenance Planning

Overall Equipment Effectiveness Simplified: Analyzing OEE to find the Improvement Opportunities

Practical Guide to FMEA : A Proactive Approach to Failure Analysis

Toyota Healthcare: 7+1 Types Of Waste

The Ultimate Guide to Successful Lean Transformation: Top Reasons Why Companies Fail to Achieve and Sustain Excellence through Lean Improvement

Kanban the Toyota Way: An Inventory Buffering System to Eliminate Inventory

Risk Assessment Using FMEA: A Case of Reliable Improvement

The Problem Solving Kata as a Tool for Culture Change: Building True Lean Organizations

Lean Healthcare: Enhancing the Patient Care Process while Eliminating Waste and Lowering Costs

Heijunka: The Leveling Art of the Japanese Auto Industry

Creating a One-Piece Flow and Production Cell: Just-in-time Production with Toyota's Single Piece Flow

Watch for more at https://www.personal-lean.org/.

About the Author

Mohammed Hamed Ahmed Soliman is an industrial engineer, consultant, university lecturer, operational excellence leader, and author. He works as a lecturer at the American University in Cairo and as a consultant for several international industrial organizations. Soliman earned a bachelor of science in Engineering and a master's degree in Quality Management. He earned post-graduate degrees in Industrial Engineering and Engineering Management. He holds numerous certificates in management, industry, quality, and cost engineering. For most of his career, Soliman worked as a regular employee for various industrial sectors. This included crystal-glass making, fertilizers, and chemicals. He did this while educating people about the culture of continuous improvement. Soliman has lectured at Princess Noura University and trained the maintenance team in Vale Oman Pelletizing Company. He has been lecturing at

The American University in Cairo for 8 years and has designed and delivered 40 leadership and technical skills enhancement training modules. Soliman is a member at the Institute of Industrial and Systems Engineers and a member with the Society for Engineering and Management Systems. He has published several articles in peer reviewed academic journals and magazines. His writings on lean manufacturing, leadership, productivity, and business appear in Industrial Engineers, Lean Thinking, Industrial Management, and Sage Publications. Soliman's blog is www.personal-lean.org.

Read more at https://www.personal-lean.org/.

personal-lean.org

About the Publisher

Personal-lean is dedicated to publish high quality educational content, assessment, training in the filed of business for various industrial sectors. And is a growing educational organization, with products and services in various countries.